TARDIGI

C000076603

The Ultimate Guide on
All You Need to Know
About the Water Bear

Alex J. Morgan

Table of Contents

CHAPTER ONE

TARDIGRADE OVERVIEW

Tardigrades, often referred to as "water bears" or "moss piglets," are microscopic, water-residing animals belonging to the phylum Tardigrada. They are acknowledged for their fantastic resilience and potential to survive extreme environmental situations that might be lethal to so many other organisms. Few records of tardigrades:

Body Size: Tardigrades are very small, normally ranging in size from approximately 0.1 to as a minimum 1.5 millimeters in length. They may be visible beneath a microscope, and their appearance is frequently defined as corresponding to an obese, 8-legged endure.

Immoderate Resilience:

Tardigrades are famous for his or her capacity to live on extreme situations. They can withstand severe temperatures (each excessive and low), excessive strain, radiation, or even the vacuum of area. They gain this with the aid of entering a kingdom called cryptobiosis, wherein they dry out and curl up, essentially setting their metabolism on keep. This kingdom lets in them to live to tell the tale harsh conditions for prolonged periods and "come back to existence" while situations enhance.

Dehydration and Rehydration: Tardigrades can undergo desiccation (extreme drying out) by way of manner of stepping into the cryptobiotic kingdom. Whilst rehydrated, they can resume everyday activities inner hours or days.

Feeding mechanism: Tardigrades are usually microphages; this means that they feed on small particles and microorganisms. They use their stylets (sharp, needle-like mouthparts) to pierce cells and suck out their contents.

food plan

Tardigrades are microorganisms that commonly feed on a weight loss program of small particles and microorganisms. Their feeding behavior are tailored to their microscopic length and clean digestive machine. Here's an healthy eating plan:

Microphagy: Tardigrades are taken into consideration microphagous, which means they eat very small food debris. Their mouthparts, referred to as the buccal apparatus, are tailored for piercing and sucking fluids from their meal assets.

Weight-reduction plan Composition: Tardigrades feed on a diffusion of substances, along with plant cells, algae, bacteria, and extraordinary microorganisms present in their habitat. They're particularly not unusual in habitats wealthy in organic rely, together with mosses, lichens, and leaf clutter.

Tardigrades use their stylets, which can be needle-like structures inside their buccal system, to pierce person cells or small organisms. They inject digestive enzymes after which suck up the liquified contents of their prey.

Prey choice: Tardigrades are opportunistic feeders, meaning they eat anything small organisms are available of their environment. Their diet can range primarily based on the correct habitat they inhabit.

Aquatic Feeding: In aquatic environments, tardigrades feed on algae, bacteria, and unique microorganisms suspended within the water. They use their stylets to pierce cells or seize debris from the encircling water.

Terrestrial Feeding: In terrestrial habitats, tardigrades feed on plant cells, algae, and microorganisms found in wet environments. They are generally associated with mosses and lichens, in which they inhabit the areas among plant cells.

Digestive device: Tardigrades have an entire digestive tool, such as a mouth, pharynx, esophagus, intestine, and anus. After ingesting their food, it's far broken down within the digestive tract, and nutrients are absorbed for energy and boom.

Feeding technique in Cryptobiosis: whilst tardigrades enter cryptobiosis (a country of suspended animation), their metabolic tactics are substantially slowed down or halted. During this country, they do no longer feed. Their capacity to go into cryptobiosis is one of the motives they may stay on in extreme situations.

Tardigrades' feeding habits make contributions to their function in numerous ecosystems, wherein they take part in nutrient cycling and have interaction with exceptional microorganisms. Even as their feeding technique is extraordinarily clean, it plays an essential position in their survival and ability to evolve to awesome environments.

CHAPTER TWO

BODILY TENDENCIES

Tardigrades own a fixed of unique bodily characteristics that cause them to charming microscopic creatures. Here are the vital aspect bodily tendencies of tardigrades:

Length: Tardigrades are very small animals, typically starting from 0.1 to at least 1.5 millimeters in length. Some species can be even smaller, whilst a few big species can achieve up to 2.5 millimeters.

Segmented body: Tardigrades have an exceptional body shape which includes three segments: a head, a three-segmented trunk, and a hind phase. Each of these segments serves particular features and includes various inner organs.

Outside Cuticle: The outermost layer of a tardigrade's body is blanketed by using a defensive cuticle. This cuticle includes chitin, a tough and bendy material. The cuticle permits the tardigrade keep moisture and provides some diploma of safety.

Legs: Tardigrades are diagnosed for their eight legs, each completing in claws or adhesive pads. The ones legs are jointed and ready with muscular tissues, allowing the tardigrade to move with a distinct sluggish, lumbering gait.

Tardigrades have a specialized mouthpart referred to as a "buccal gadget." This mouthpart includes a couple of stylets (needle-like systems) that can be prolonged to pierce and suck fluids from plant cells and small organisms, which make up their weight-reduction plan.

Plump look: Tardigrades frequently have a plump and round appearance because of the manner they're capable of inflate their own bodies with water. Whilst hydrated, they make bigger, and after they lose water, they settlement and assume a wrinkled appearance.

Eyespots:

some tardigrades have easy eyespots that can come across mild, even though their imaginative and prescient is exceedingly easy. The ones eyespots help them sense adjustments in mild situations, which may be important for their survival in their habitats.

Water Vascular tool:

Tardigrades have a clean water vascular device that allows them circulate fluids in the direction in their own bodies. This gadget aids in meting out nutrients and gases and performs a position in osmoregulation.

Intestine and Digestion:
Tardigrades have a complete digestive machine, which includes a mouth, pharynx, esophagus, gut, and anus. They use their stylets to pierce plant cells and exceptional small organisms to extract nutrients.

Tardigrades have specific adaptations that permit them to live on severe dehydration thru methods like anhydrobiosis and cryptobiosis. Within the direction of those states, they curl up and input a suspended animation mode, efficaciously shutting down their metabolism till they rehydrate.

Those bodily traits together make contributions to the survival and adaptability of tardigrades in several environments, especially in situations wherein many different organisms might struggle or perish because of intense conditions.

CHAPTER THREE

Creation and reproduction

Tardigrades reproduce through sexual replica, with women and men usually gift. They lay eggs, which hatch into juvenile tardigrades that resemble miniature variations of the adults.

Extra than 1,000 species had been advised from numerous habitats which encompass marine, glowing water or limno-terrestrial environments. All tardigrades require surrounding water to develop and reproduce, but some species—commonly the ones living within the limno-terrestrial environments—have the potential to tolerate nearly whole dehydration. Even as encountering desiccation, tolerant tardigrades lose body water and enter a reduced in size dehydrated usually referred to as anhydrobiosis, that's a reversible ametabolic nation. The dehydrated tardigrades withstand an enormous range of bodily extremes that commonly disallow the survival of maximum organisms, including severe temperatures (from $-273\,^{\circ}\mathrm{C}$ to almost $100\,^{\circ}\mathrm{C}$), excessive stress

(7.5 GPa), immersion in organic solvent, exposure to high dose of irradiation or even direct exposure to open space9. Despite the fact that such uncommon tolerance of some tardigrades has lengthy interested researchers, the molecular mechanisms permitting such awesome tolerance have remained largely unknown.

Courtship and Mating: The technique of mating in tardigrades regularly involves courtship behaviors. Male tardigrades can also use their stylets (mouthparts) to softly interact with girls, and chemical cues may play a function in attracting capability buddies.

Sperm transfer: for the duration of mating, adult males switch sperm to ladies. Tardigrades have specialized tubular systems known as "spermatophores" that consist of sperm. The ones spermatophores are produced by using the guys and are frequently related to or left within the surroundings.

Fertilization: After receiving sperm from a male, the woman stores the sperm in her reproductive tract. Fertilization happens internally, and the fertilized eggs boom inside the lady's body.

Egg Laying: as quickly as the fertilized eggs have advanced sufficiently, the female lays the eggs. The eggs are regularly laid within the environment, normally in a secure location that offers protection from functionality threats.

Improvement:

The eggs hatch into juvenile tardigrades, which resemble miniature variations of the adults. Those juveniles go through a chain of molts as they grow, dropping their exoskeletons to cope with their increasing size.

Lifestyles Cycle and boom:

as the juveniles maintain to molt and broaden, they frequently mature into adults. Tardigrades commonly have a fantastically quick lifestyles span, with a few species living for only a few weeks to three months.

It is well worth noting that whilst sexual duplicate is the number one mode of reproduction in tardigrades, there's additionally some evidence of parthenogenesis, a form of reproduction in which ladies can produce offspring without mating. But sexual replica is more commonplace and giant for the genetic variety of the population.

Regular, the reproduction approach in tardigrades contributes to the survival and continuation in their species in diverse habitats, even inside the face of hard environmental conditions.

CHAPTER FOUR

CLINICAL SIGNIFICANCE OF TARDIGRADE

Tardigrades were identified to be the most indestructible animal on earth. They can live to tell the story on vacuum of region for a long time, continue to exist excessive harsh situations close to lava, live on underwater with big air pressure or even on a given time period inner stomach intestines.

Their life isn't always in fact seemed, but tardigrades are capable of stop their metabolism and emerge as immortal (nation cryptobiosis). Tardigrades or water bears have been found in an ice sheet 2,000 years and came returned to lifestyles. This shape of resistance lets in it to droop time, but also to stay to tell the tale intense temperatures. Tardigrades don't certainly age however, their lifespan tiers from 3–4 months for a few species, up to two years for other species.

That is vital to scientists because they need to have a take a look at how and why their metabolism lets in them to live to inform the story in immoderate harsh situations without hurting themselves and the way they react to positive guy-made harsh environments to in addition their have a examine that permits them in environmental conditions to stay on dehydration, desiccation, freezing, and oxygen deficiency. Inside the cryptobiotic nation, all measurable metabolic techniques save you, stopping reproduction, improvement, and restore. Our metabolism is constantly converting because of our genetics. If people sooner or later are to postpone growing antique consequences and even become partly biologically immortal, reading Hydras, Jellyfish, lobsters, and tardigrades body cells are the remarkable form of start.

Cryonics patients are cared for in the expectation that future generation, particularly molecular nanotechnology, might be to be had to contrary harm related to the cryonics process. tardigrades play a vital feature to locating out and bringing again frozen cells to lifestyles without harm. Information their lifestyles techniques can be critical for remedy, biotechnology or astrobiology. Personal studies and funding in stem cells is growing that appears over what causes growing older and its outcomes in fine brief/long term molecular states.

Tardigrades are microscopic creatures which have managed to continue to exist on this Earth for over six hundred million years. They have got survived extremes of heat and cold and now have the potential to dry out and are available again to life. For this reason, they may be being studied through scientists. Their particular abilities might be used to keep other biological materials, which include blood cells in blood banks or in the direction of engineering plants that can resist severe temperatures.

GENETIC VARIETY

Tardigrades have a various sort of genetic diversifications that make a contribution to their survival abilities. A number of their genes are notion to play a function in protective their cells from harm as a result of extreme situations.

Genetic version

Tardigrades, moreover known as water bears, are small aquatic animals having four pairs of leg. Some tardigrade species tolerate almost entire dehydration and show off great tolerance to numerous physical extremes within the dehydrated nation. Here we determine a first-rate genome collection of Ramazzottius varieornatus, one of the maximum strain-tolerant tardigrade species. Specific gene repertoire analyses show the presence of a small proportion (1.2% or much less) of putative remote places genes, loss of gene pathways that sell stress damage, growth of gene families

32

associated with ameliorating harm, and evolution and immoderate expression of novel tardigrade-particular proteins. Minor adjustments inside the gene expression profiles sooner or later of dehydration and rehydration propose constitutive expression of tolerance-related genes. The use of human cultured cells, we reveal that a tardigrade-precise DNA-associating protein suppresses X-ray-induced DNA harm with the aid of the use of ~forty% and improves radiotolerance. The ones findings mean the relevance of tardigrade-unique proteins to tolerability and tardigrades can be a bountiful supply of new safety genes and mechanisms.

Medical significance:

Tardigrades have captured the interest of scientists and researchers due to their particular resilience and capability programs in numerous fields. Their potential to live to tell the story intense situations has led to investigate on how their survival mechanisms might be applied to areas which consist of area excursion, medication, and conservation.

In latest years, tardigrades have received reputation in popular lifestyle and have grown to be a symbol of intense resilience and adaptability. Their potential to endure situations that is probably deadly to most different organisms has sparked fascination and scientific research.

CHAPTER FIVE

HABITAT:

Tardigrades are determined in a diffusion of habitats, consisting of soil, leaf clutter, mosses, lichens, and aquatic environments. They may be located in both terrestrial and marine ecosystems.

Tardigrades are a substitute adaptable microorganism that may be located in a huge sort of habitats round the arena. Their capability to stay to inform the story excessive situations contributes to their presence in various environments. Here's a pinnacle stage view in their habitat and distribution:

Terrestrial Habitats:

• Soil: Tardigrades are normally decided in soil, mainly in the top layers wherein moisture is gift. They play a function in soil ecosystems via feeding on microorganisms and participating in nutrient biking.

•   Mosses and Lichens: Tardigrades are frequently associated with mosses and lichens. They inhabit the areas among plant cells, wherein they feed on algae and microorganism.

•   Leaf muddle: Fallen leaves at the woodland ground create a wet microenvironment appropriate for tardigrades. They may be located inside the wet layers of leaf muddle.

Aquatic Habitats:

•   Freshwater: Tardigrades inhabit diverse freshwater environments, collectively with lakes, ponds, rivers, and streams.

They are specially sufficient in areas with excessive stages of natural be counted and flowers.

intense Temperatures:

Tardigrades are capable of surviving both excessive and coffee temperatures. They're able to go through freezing temperatures similarly to immoderate warmth.

- **barren place Environments**: fine tardigrades are tailored to continue to exist in arid wilderness regions. They make use of cryptobiosis to undergo dehydration and might rehydrate while water will become available.

• excessive Altitudes: Tardigrades were determined at high altitudes, such as on mountain peaks. Their resilience to radiation and immoderate cold possibly contributes to their presence in such places.

• Polar regions: Tardigrades had been located in Antarctica and distinctive polar regions. They might live on in the extreme bloodless and are frequently associated with mosses and lichens.

• Microscopic Ecosystems: Tardigrades may be discovered in microhabitats internal normal environments, which encompass in tree bark, underneath rocks, and in damp corners.

The distribution of tardigrades is full-size and no longer restricted to precise geographic regions. They were documented on all continents, which incorporates Antarctica. Their first-rate functionality to go into cryptobiosis permits them to persist in difficult environments and disperse over lengthy distances thru several method, consisting of wind, water currents, and hitchhiking on extraordinary organisms.

The end

Printed in Great Britain
by Amazon

ELEPHANTS, ECONOMICS AND IVORY

ELEPHANTS, ECONOMICS AND IVORY

Edward B. Barbier
Joanne C. Burgess
Timothy M. Swanson
David W. Pearce

Earthscan Publications Ltd   London

DEDICATION

We dedicate this book to all who love elephants, and especially
Lara Helen Barbier
Emma Louise Burgess
Nicholas Gorz Swanson
Susan Pearce

First published in 1990 by
Earthscan Publications Ltd
3 Endsleigh Street, London WC1H 0DD

British Library Cataloguing in Publication Data
Barbier, Edward B
  Elephants, economics and ivory
  1. African elephants. Conservation
  I. Title   II. Burgess, J. C.   III. Swanson, T. M.
  IV. Pearce, D. W.

ISBN 1-85383-073-9

Cover designed by David King
Production by David Williams Associates (081-521 4130)
Typeset by DP Photosetting, Aylesbury, Bucks
Printed and bound by Guernsey Press Co. Ltd, Guernsey, C.I.

Earthscan Publications Ltd is a wholly owned and editorially
independent subsidiary of the International Institute for
Environment and Development (IIED).